TABLE OF CONTENTS

Introduction	2
Tips for More Engagement	6
Daily Account Tasks	10
Settings	12
Profile	23
Pinned Tweet	26
Twitter Dashboard	29
Retweets	35
Replies	37
Hashtags	38
Building Your Followers	41
Cleaning Up Your Account	44
Making Local and National Lists	45

Hello twitter enthusiasts and thank you for jumping aboard. My name is Cynthia Schmidt and I am a landlord/real estate investor.My husband, Gary and I are authors and teachers of the nationwide program Collect Back Rent Training Course for Landlords. We developed the Collect Back Rent Course 15 years ago to educate the landlords on judgment collection. We have traveled to 37 states and 50 REIA groups to present our Collect Back Rent. There have been 3,000 landlords that have taken our course and getting the money they deserve. We have been on this mission for 15 years and it has been rewarding.

About 8 years ago we decided to reduce the miles on the road and start selling on the internet. When I first joined twitter I felt like I was spinning my wheels. I didn't know how to connect with landlords. I started following the social media marketing profiles that had a 100k followers. That definitely was not the right path to get to the real estate investors and landlords. The tweets were coming in strong with social marketing and pushing their product. The messages I received from the marketers were automated and definitely spamming.

On a rainy Sunday I went through my account and unfollowed all the social media marketing profiles. By doing this procedure I developed a cleaning up my account routine.

I made an all out search for all real estate minded twitter profiles and started following. It could be plumbers, appraisers, landlords, real estate investors, painters and real estate agents. Their real estate tweets gave me valuable information to share to my followers. I would click on the link to the articles and blogs to learn more about real estate.

I could see my posts were being retweeted and liked so I knew I was on the right track. Finally, I was building a twitter account with qualified real estate followers.

Keeping the focus on my goal of engagement and selling my product.

Most of the profiles I followed were real estate agents because some were landlords and the content fit my business. And there are 10 times more realtors on twitter than landlords so I could keep my account spinning.

What is spinning your account? Every time you go to your account it shows action. New followers. likes and retweets everday means it is spinning.

Jump ahead 8 years and I have over 8,000 realtors in my 10k qualified real estate followers. During the 8 years I noticed that out of all my real estate agent followers maybe 30 accounts really have it going on. The usual tweet from the realtors were "I would love to show you my listing" and I would notice with no engagements. Clicking over to their profiles I also noticed that the average account had around 50 followers with following around 100. The accounts were somewhat dormant and needed a shot of energy and knowledge.

This was telling me that the realtors needed training when it came to Twitter. Not only with their postings but to build their accounts with local and national followers.

That is why I wrote the books, courses and managing twitter accounts right to the realtors. I realized that their time is valuable and they want to sell homes.

Having a blueprint to follow everyday to make your Twitter experience a money making venture.

If you are trying sell a product or your business:

Don't post politics. It is hard enough to sell without eliminating 50 percent of your potential customers. One of my longtime realtor associates put out ugly politic posts and I unfollowed her. Gary and I bought 50 homes from her realty business. If I knew her bad attitude before I bought the homes-she won't have gotten one sale. When I see numerous political tweets from an account I unfollow. I am not going to get in a spit fight on social media over politics.

Tweet frequently and about your subject. If your subject is real estate I would suggest sticking to it. The goal of your tweets is to drive them to the website. Facebook is great for sharing pictures of your children and food but I don't see the clicks to the website.

Optimize your posting time. **After studying the "Learn to be a Twitter Expert" you will definitely be utilizing the posting time.**

So many profiles are spinning their wheels with the "Hope and Post" mentality. Trying to find out why they are on twitter. Every business twitter account needs direction and training to move forward. Nothing feels better than coming to your account and seeing new qualified followers, retweets and replies.

Post visual content. **Photos, gifs and videos to gain the needed attention. I suggest putting out powerful videos with music to grab their attention. You can download your videos on Vimeo or You-tube on an MP4 then share it on twitter.**

Be sure to introduce your new follower **to your following. The automated "Hey ____ thank you for the follow" goes nowhere. I know it is trending the word "Hey" but I don't like it. You want to make them feel special in your network.**

Tweet during weekends and peak hours: **People are most likely to remain active on social media during weekends as they are generally off of work. Peak time during weekdays is in the afternoon, somewhere between** 12 pm to 3 pm, **as people have their lunch breaks in that time period.**

Being able to find out when your target audience is the most active, you will get more views and the Twitter engagement rate will increase.

DAILY TASKS

1 Check notifications: **This is where I start my account daily. I always show appreciation to the followers who retweeted, replied and just followed me. When one of my followers retweets one of my posts, I return the favor. I take the time to look over their profile and retweet one of their posts. All my followers are special and I learn so much from their posts. When they realize that you want to engage they will follow the pattern.**

2 New followers: **Not all new followers fit into your real estate mode. Learn to monitor your account. You don't have to follow everyone and you can certainly block unfavorable accounts. Buying followers isn't a good idea. I can tell by looking at an account that bought followers**

3. Engage with old & new followers: **Retweets, hashtags, shout outs, replies & quotes. This is what gets your account buzzing. Each time one of your followers retweets your post-it goes to all of their followers. This is the big difference between twitter and other networks, there is more sharing of posts**

I feel the *cherry on the sundae is a retweet with a comment*. It is great that you retweeted but that extra effort of a comment pays off. That extra effort will be noticed by your followers and appreciated, I rarely just "like" a post.

4. Follow new real estate minded accounts everyday-I average about 20 new followers a day. Constantly scoping out all the real estate accounts for retweets and new followers. Your account is not going to keep growing if you stop following new people.

5. Tweet about your listings but you will need to engage to grow your account: **"I would love to show you my listing" goes nowhere. I have seen hundreds of realtor's post with this heading. Post about your listings but tucked in with real estate education posts. You have got to engage your followers or I call it tweeting alone. Is anyone out there?**

SETTINGS

Home-Timeline displays a stream of tweets from accounts you have chosen to follow on twitter.

Explore The Explore tab is more useful than the Moments tab because Explore has more information. Explore also includes Trends, Search, Moments and Explore All. Each has a preview of the top listings and you can tap "More" to see a longer list. Popular videos or tweets are at the top of the Explore

Trends-If you are looking to see what is trending on Twitter, you will find it at the top of the Explore If you are looking in Twitter for the search icon, a magnifying glass, you will not find it in the main section.

TWITTER MOMENTS

Moments-**The Moments feature has not gone away. Instead, Moments is found in the Explore tab below Trends. Moments is a collection of what Twitter views as important tweets on trending topics.**

Notifications-**I check my notifications the first thing when I hit my account. I can see my followers and engagement of my tweets.You can get notifications for things like direct messages, follows, likes, replies to your tweets, mentions, and retweets of your tweets. Check or uncheck the boxes for the notifications you wish to receive. Click on sidebar "More" then and go to privacy.and settings. Click notifications and you can determine what notifications you wll receive.**

Messages

If I receive a message that I feel is not in the real estate mode, this is the sign I need to unfollow and/or block. I am not on twitter to meet people to date.

Usually if I stray off of my real estate followers then it seems like that is when a message comes it that rubs me wrong.

Sending messages after you have engaged with your new follower's profile is great I suggest sending a message like " Thank you for the follow *Cynthia* and if you have a chance please check out my pinned tweet. I would appreciate it".

> Good morning Realtors Digital Assistant on this March Saturday and thank you for the follow. Will be watching for your posts to share with my followers. If you have a chance if you could check out my latest tweet-that would be great, Cindy from New Mexico twitter.com/mrslandlady/st...

Your pinned tweet will have the link to your website. When I receive an automated message or spamming direct message it doesn't make me feel special.

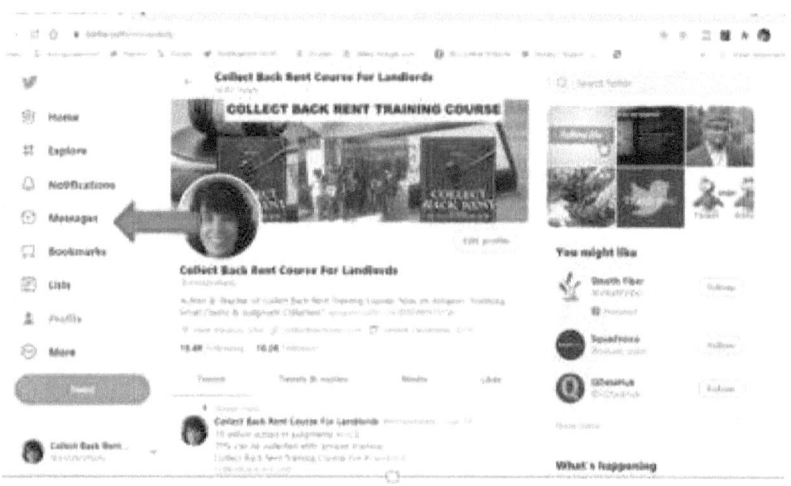

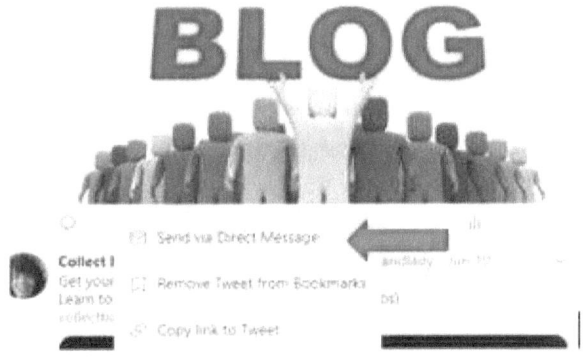

Another good way to send a direct message after engaging with your new follower is sending a tweet as the direct message.

I always copy the username and paste into the message. Your prized pinned tweet can become your message.

Be sure to make the message short and sweet. Such as "Good evening *Cynthia* on this date and thank you for the follow. If you have a chance to check out my tweet, it would be much appreciated, *Gary*"

Bookmarks

To **bookmark** a tweet click the share icon under the tweet and select, "**Add tweet to bookmarks**". To find it later, tap **bookmarks** from your profile icon menu.

You can remove tweets from your **bookmarks** at any time. Only you can see what you've **bookmarked**.

When I want to save one of the top tweets that isn't my pinned tweet, I add to bookmarks. Instead of scrolling 1,000's of my posts, I have quick access to retweet

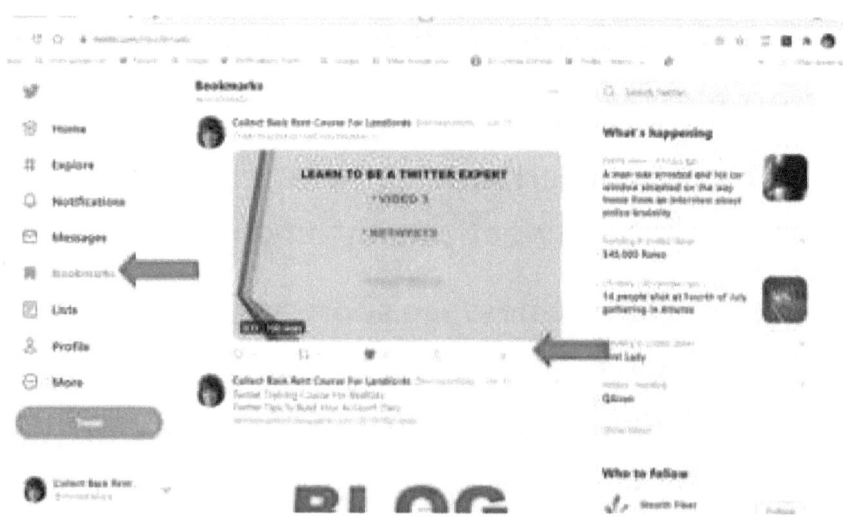

Profile

One of the most important elements of the twitter profile is that it shows a history of the last tweets the person has posted. That is probably the best indicator of how each person engages twitter.

Logging out of account

Twitter just changed the location of the logging out option. It used to be up in the right corner but it was changed to the lower left.

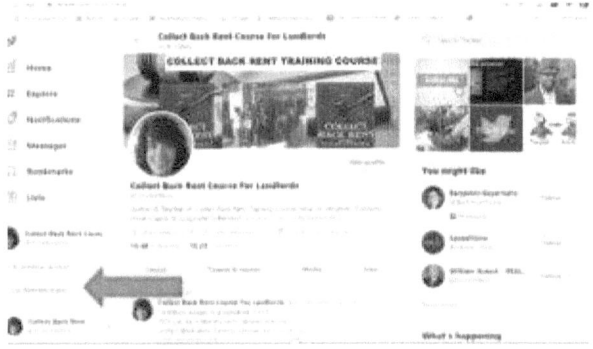

Changing username

Your username can be up to 15 characters long.
@realtor course

Your display username can be up to 50 characters long.
Collect Back Rent Course for Landlords

I suggest looking for a handle that is closest to describing your business. My Twitter Training Course for Realtors is "@realtor course" and this reflects my product. If the username is taken, you'll be prompted to choose another one.

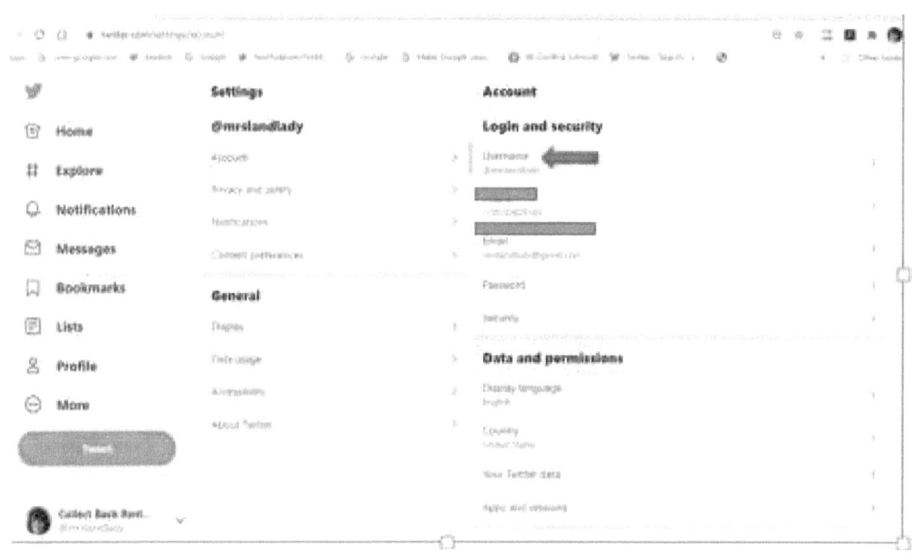

Password

I always change my password every 90 days just to protect my account.This cuts down the possibility of your account being hacked I would suggest logging out of your account then logging back in. I have managed accounts where the client gave me their password and it was incorrect. When they logged out and then back in they discovered the problem.

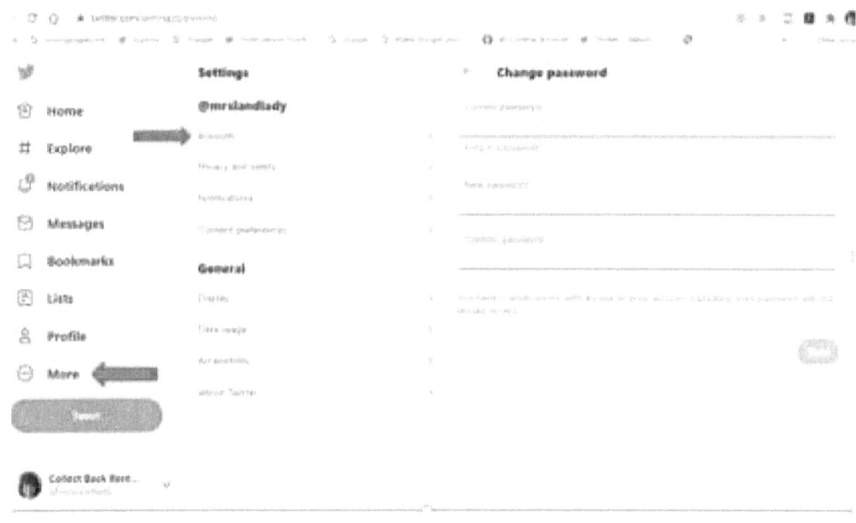

Security

To protect your account for unauthorized access by requiring a second authorization method and addition to your password.

Addition password protection can be applied but you will need to verify it with your phone number. I feel these two options will really help your account to remain safe.

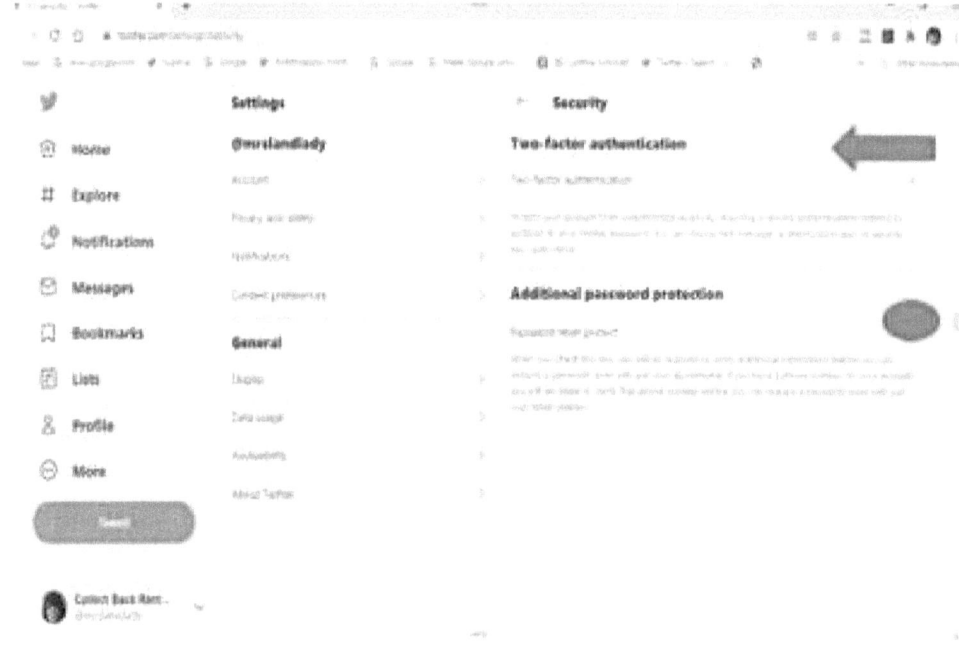

Privacy and Safety

Protecting your tweet to people who follow you is the way I have chosen. If you chose to protect your tweets, you will need to approve each new follower.

If you are selling a product then you would not protect your tweets. I rarely follow a protected account You can monitor your account by unfollowing or blocking.

I would definitely check to not receive messages from anyone on twitter. You only want messages from your followers

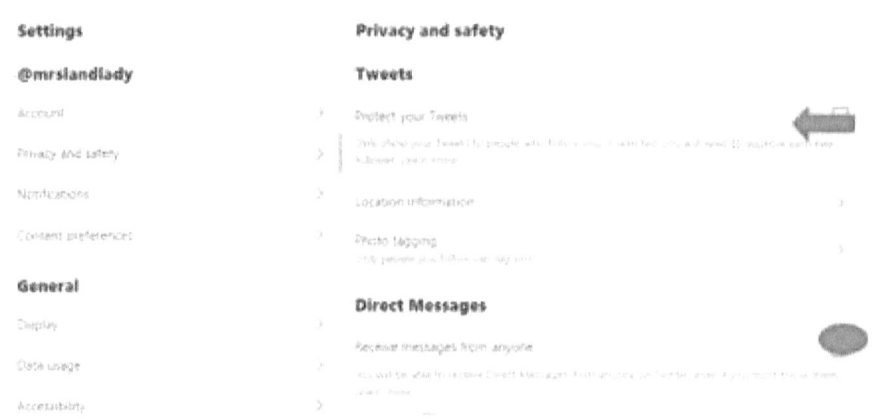

PROFILE

Editing the profile

When editing your profile you have to click "edit profile". You can upload your profile picture, header image and add details to your bio. This is very important to branding your account to reflect your business. This is the first thing your new followers will see when they are viewing your profile .You have to have a clear picture for the profile, descriptive header image and the full description of your business.

The profile is the advertisement for your business. If you advertised in a local paper or MLS magazine you would want the most information to your potential customers.

Information that should be displayed is what you are selling, where you are located and contact information (website). Many times I have viewed a real estate agent's profile and I don't know where they are located or what company they are with. When selling real estate you should always put the location on your header image, bio and tweets.

Profile Picture

The personal image uploaded to your twitter profile in the settings tab of your account. Make sure the picture is clear and a close-up. A pleasant smile definitely won't hurt the recipe.

Header Image

Sometimes people may not be familiar with your brand or what you do. The header image should have the name of your business, location, picture of subject and contact information such as your website

I created my header image on power-point presentation and filed it as a jpeg. I made sure I had all the information in the center of the slide. There are many twitter banner companies online that would do a great job.

Twitter recommend image files up to 750px wide and 200px tall. If you would like your header image to display like banner that stretches across the entire page, we recommend image files 1000px wide and 200p

Pinned tweets are tweets that stay static on the top of your profile. When people visit your profile, the pinned tweet is the first thing they see, regardless of when you tweeted it

You will be driving all your traffic to your pinned tweet which explains your business the best. I believe that the video that is downloaded on an mp4 will gain engagement.

Having your website link is a must because that is our goal. Driving the followers to your company or your website is what is going to sell homes.

Click on the inverted triangle on the top corner of the right hand side. Choose the option "pin to your profile page".

This is my pinned tweet with a video. It has 135 views and rolling.

I have noticed the big realtor accounts and they keep the same pinned tweet. I have changed mine so it is up to you. If it gets lots of engagement then I would keep it.

You can download your video to an MP4 on your YouTube channel or Vimeo.

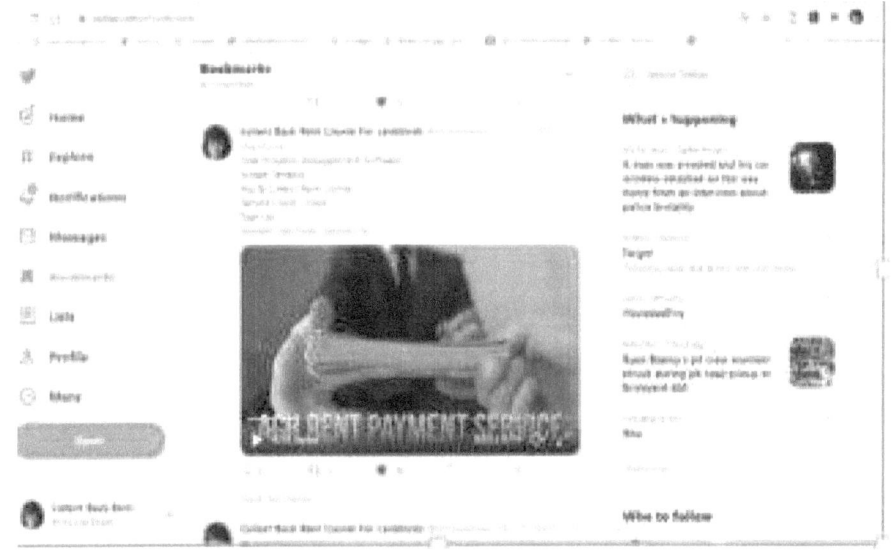

This is an affiliate of mine and I had this tweet for my pinned tweet. The tweet was up for 3 months and had 6,100 views. This is the top pinned tweet but I did spend $50 on advertisement.

There was 174 clicks from the advertisement and 32 sales. Advertising really launches your pinned tweet and you will check your analytics to determine your pinned tweet.

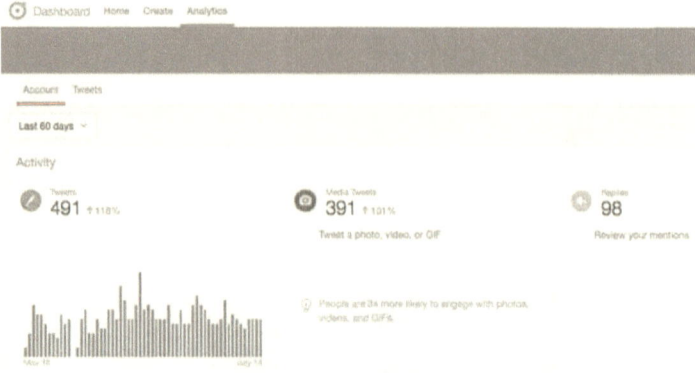

TWITTER DASHBOARD

The tweet activity dashboard is a tool you can use to learn more about your tweets. This shows the activity of your account for the month. This will determine which one of your tweets is getting engagement. We will bookmark the top tweets to refer back for circulation.

Compare your tweet activity and followers, and see how they trend over time. Click on any tweet to get a detailed view of the number of retweets, replies, likes, follows, or clicks it receives

Log into analytics.twitter.com with your twitter username and password to turn on analytics on your account. You have to turn on your analytics so you can being calculating your engagements.

ACCESSING YOUR ANALYTICS

To access your tweet activity details (on desktop or mobile), you'll need to first make sure you've logged in to analytics.twitter.com and turned on analytics for your account.

If you are having trouble accessing the tweet activity dashboard, your account may not meet one or more of the following requirements:

Account primarily Tweets in Arabic, Brazilian Portuguese, Danish, Dutch, English, Filipino, Finnish, French, German, Indonesian, Italian, Japanese, Korean, Norwegian, Russian, Simplified Chinese, Spanish, Swedish, Thai, Traditional Chinese, Turkish

Account is at least 14 days old

Account does not violate policy

Account is not deleted, restricted, or suspended

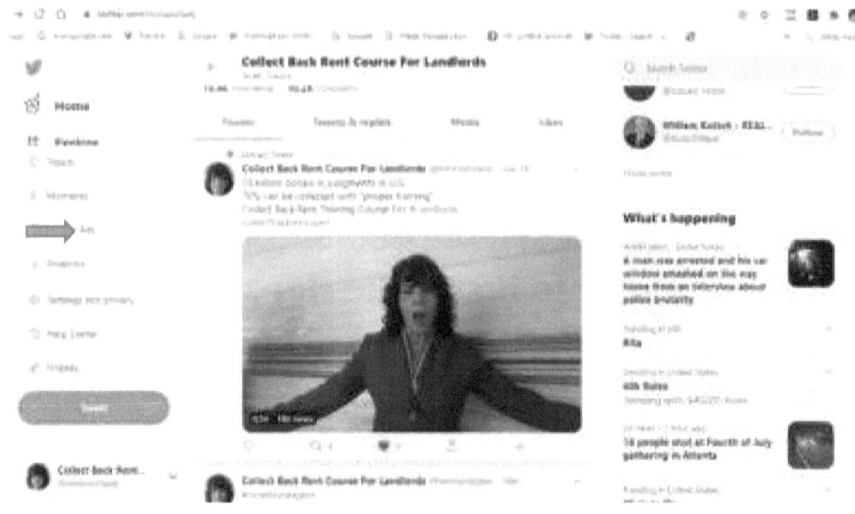

Once you have clicked on "More" then you have the analytics. Checking every week can give you an overview of your account

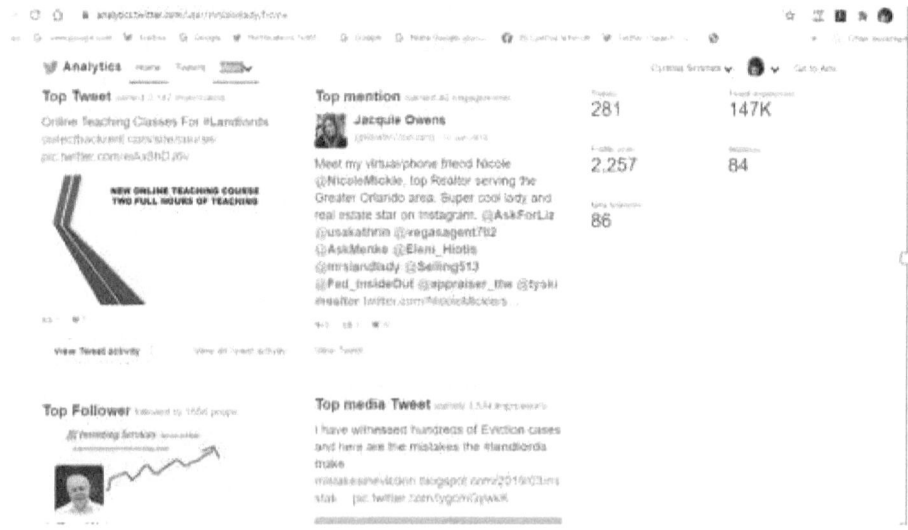

EVALUATING A PARTICULAR TWEET

Impressions-**Total tally of all the times the tweet has been seen. This includes not only the times it appears in a one of your followers' timeline but also the**

Engagements-**Media views are views on any images or videos you add to your tweets. It tells you how engaged people are with your tweets you also have to factor in retweets, replies, clicks and likes**

Total Engagements-**Total number of times a user interacted with a tweet. Clicks anywhere on the tweet, including retweets, replies, follows, likes, links, cards, hashtags, embedded media, username, profile photo, or tweet expansion.**

Engagement rate: **Number of engagements divided by impressions.**

Media clicks: **Clicks to view a photo or video in the** tweet

Detail expands: **Clicks on the Tweet to view more details**
Embedded media clicks: Clicks to view a photo or video
in the Tweet. Engagements: Total number of times a
user interacted with a Tweet.

Likes: **Times a user liked the tweet.**

Link clicks: **Clicks on a URL or Card in the tweet link
clicks. This is a big one for my account because that is
potential sales of my product.**

Replies: **Times a user replied to the tweet. When two
people are replying to one another, only relevant
people, such as those who follow the person who
replied and the person in the conversation, will see
the reply in their timeline.**

Retweets: **Times a user retweeted the tweet. Shared via
email: times a user emailed the tweet to someone.
When a follower retweets I send a retweet with a
comment to circulate the tweet.**

I always check my tweets by accessing the analytics. This helps me monitor which tweets to add to my bookmarks which is easily accessible. I can easily determine which tweet will be my pinned tweet

The most important part of the tweet for me is the number of clicks to my website or amazon author page.

When they click the link I have an opportunity for sales of my manuals and courses.

My goal on twitter is to engage with my followers and sell my product. If I don't get many clicks then I won't add it to the bookmarks or my pinned tweet.

RETWEETS

Retweeting is one of the big reasons I prefer Twitter to the other social platforms. When the post is retweeted on Twitter it goes to all the retweeter's followers.

I have a large Facebook page but when I post they rarely share it. They may like, love or comment but they fail to share.

My Linkedin account has over 6,000 qualified real estate connections and the same thing occurs. I will post and again they will like or comment by sharing is very limited.

RETWEETS WITH COMMENTS

A Tweet that you share publicly with your followers is known as a retweet. This is a great way to pass along news and interesting discoveries on twitter

Retweet or Retweet with comment will reference the tweet you are sharing.

REPLIES

A reply is a response to another person's tweet. You can reply by clicking or tapping the reply icon from a tweet. When you reply to someone else, your tweet will show the message

I have retweeted and liked on realtor.com and have had no engagement from the account. When I reply by clicking on the article for information with adding a picture, the account liked my reply. This keeps your account fresh so it isn't just retweeting or liking.

HASHTAGS

We use the hashtag symbol (#) before a relevant keyword or phrase in your tweet to categorize those tweets and help them show more easily in twitter search. Clicking or tapping on a hash tagged word in any message shows you other tweets that include that hashtag. Hashtags can be included anywhere in a tweet.

I rarely use more than 2 hashtags in my tweets. When I see a tweet with tons of hashtags I am not impressed. The tweet should clean and fresh with a hashtag and the link to your website.

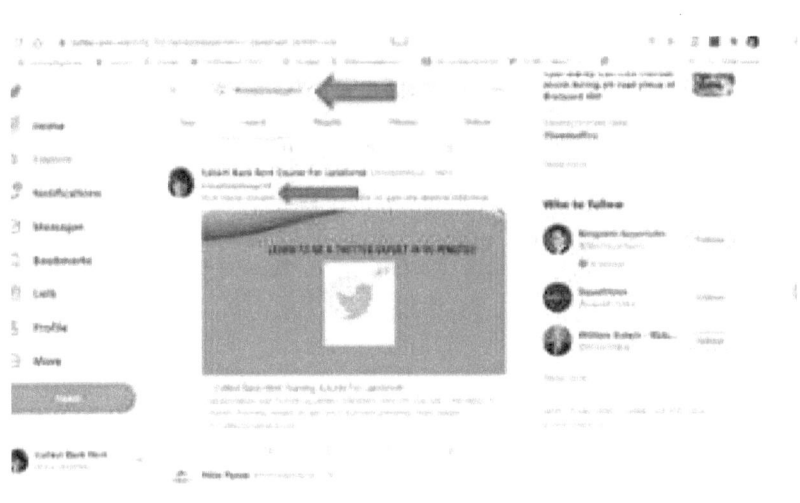

Searching for your hashtags

Twitter Search-You can also enter #your hashtag into the Twitter search box to see a real-time list of tweets that are using your tag.

Then click on latest tweets at the top of the page and there it is.

You can also check out the other accounts on that page and start following the qualified real estate people.

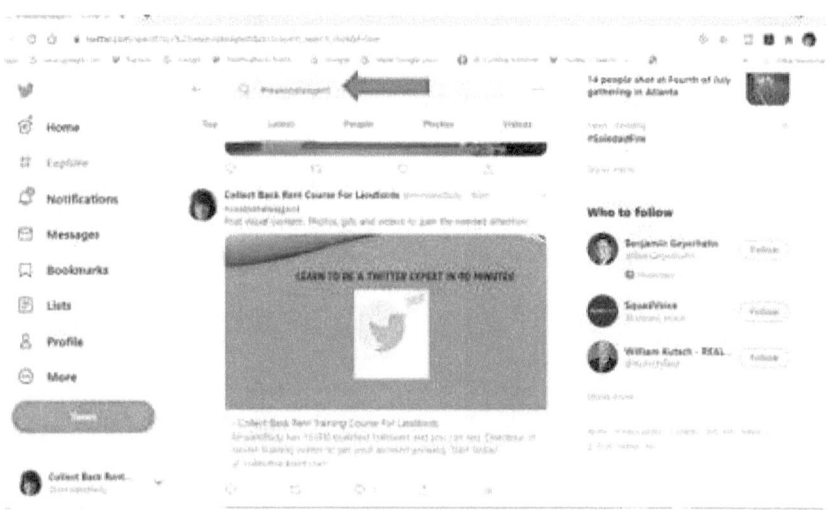

Many times I introduce my new follower with a shoutout tweet. Copy and pasting their profile information into my tweet and adding #shoutout. The new follower really appreciates your added engagement when you shout them out. You will search for your #shoutout page which gives all your new followers more needed attention.

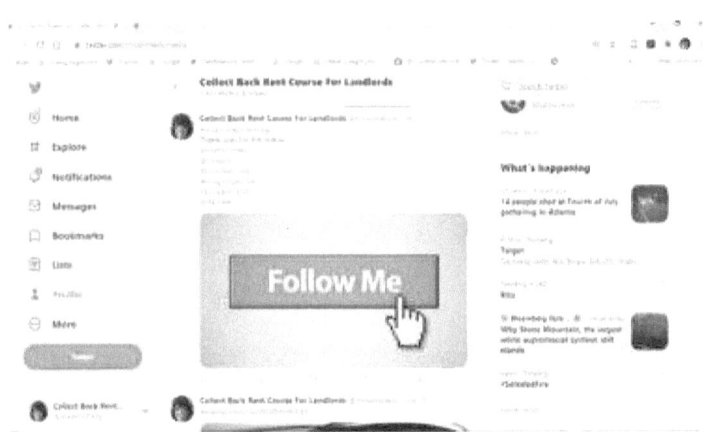

BUILDING YOUR ACCOUNT

I check my twitter account about everyday excluding holidays for new followers. I also go to these accounts to click on their new followers during the night.

Realtor.com

Realtor Magazine

National Association of Realtors

Zillow

Trulia

Remax

Another great way to build your account is to go to these accounts and notice their tweets. The example on the next page is a post by realtor.com It has 11 retweets and 18 likes. I wll click on the date in the upper right corner and it will take you to the next page, Click retweets and likes and this gives you a insight to the active tweeter engagers

realtor.com @realtordotcom · Jun 30

Built in 2011, this home in Alaska is a massive 'Peter Pan'-themed mansion!
Peek inside: rltor.cm/vc5jw

Pan'-themed mansion! Peek inside: rltor.cm/vc5jw

Jun 30 · Khoros Marketing

11 Retweets 18 Likes

COPYING THE LINK TO SHARE

One of my favorite tips on twitter is copying the link on real estate videos and sharing it on a tweet. You can put a nice hashtag such as #hometips #realestate

Instead of retweeting the tweet it goes onto your profile as your tweet and sharing the video. I always check out Bob Vila, Realtor.com or #realestate then click on videos. It gives your followers information and it is colorful

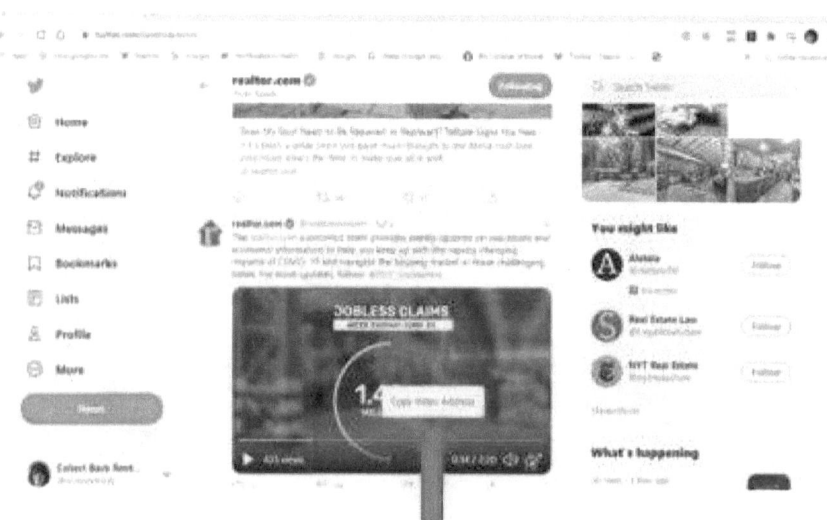

CLEANING UP YOUR ACCOUNT

I clean up my account every week and try to keep the following about 200 to 300 ahead of my followers.

I will scroll down about 100 profiles and then unfollow the ones who didn't follow me.

When I reach the following that is following me back then I know it is cleaned up. I leave about 100 accounts I am following so they have time to follow back. When I follow them and they don't follow back it creates a one way conversation.

BUILDING YOUR LISTS

A list is a curated group of twitter accounts. You can create your own list or subscribe to lists created by others. Viewing list timeline will show you a stream of tweets from only the accounts on that list. The simplified version is that twitter lists organize your twitter followers.

LOCAL

This is really important when you are selling locally. We will do an advanced search of the people in your area and start following the qualified. Make a specific list for your local followers with a title, picture and description that explains list. Go to the list everyday and engage in their tweets and they will do the same

NATIONAL

If you are selling nationwide and want to get a list going that is great. This is a way to keep your followers in the loop.

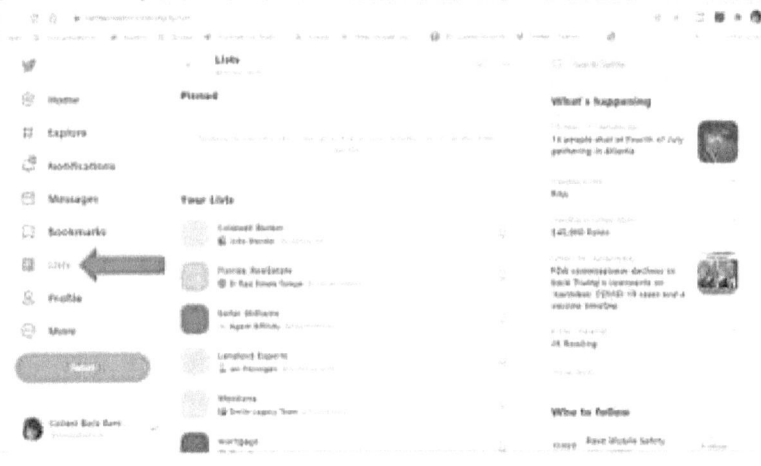

Create a new List

Name

Tampa Realtors-Investors

Description

Selling and buying real estate in Tampa Florida

Make private

How to Use Twitter Lists

This can very good because your tweets will go up on the lists. The other members of the list can access your tweets from the list. They might not be on at the time you tweeted but it is keep on the list. Naturally, there is less people on the list than your home feed.

I also check all the subscribers and this is a mega following field. This is one of the keys to building your account. Check your lists daily and it will keep your account rolling. If you don't like the list you were added to you can exit the list by clicking "unfollow"

Property Management

Property managers, management companies, apartment communities, HOA, COA Gurus, Advisors, Consult

⊝ **Dave Kinkade** @HomeLocators

72 Members   **21** Followers

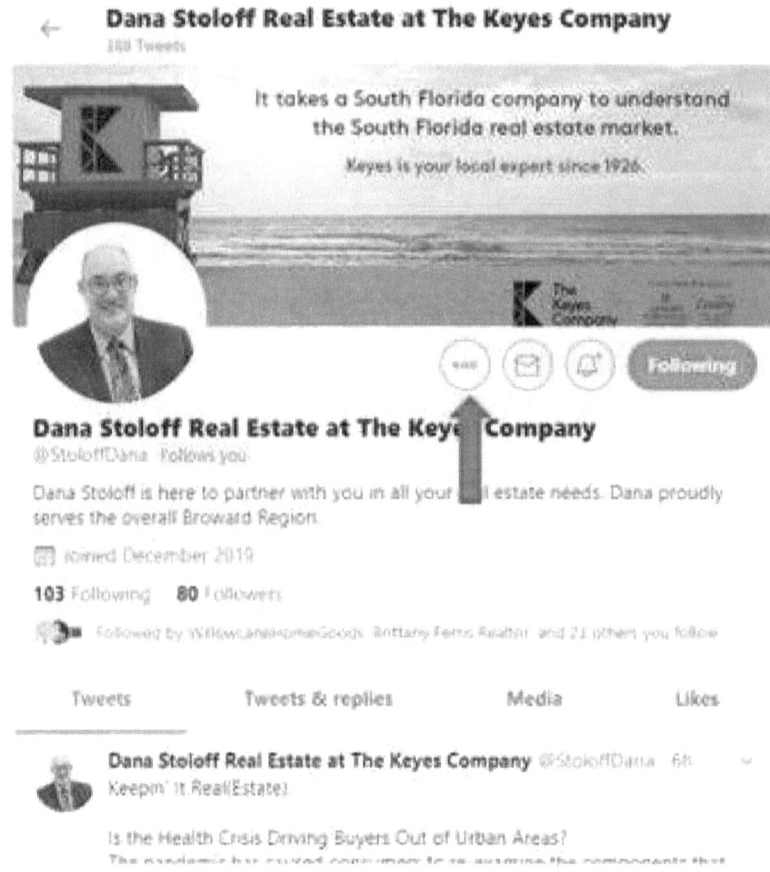

I am adding Dana to my list and I have sent a message asking his permission. This works well because most of the people want to be added.

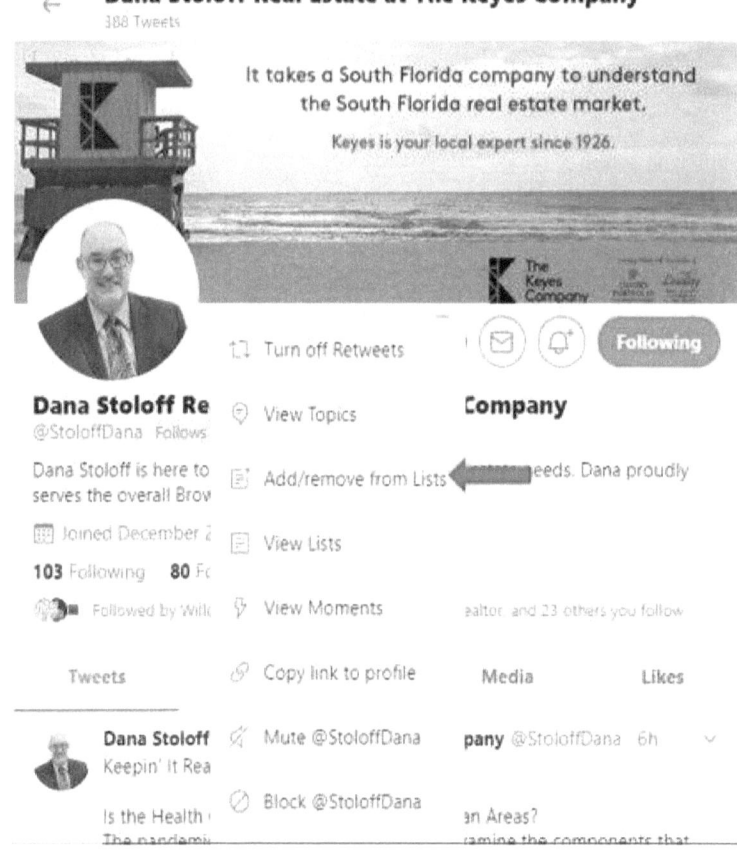

Dana Stoloff Real Estate at The Keyes Company
388 Tweets

It takes a South Florida company to understand the South Florida real estate market.

Keyes is your local expert since 1926.

The Keyes Company

↻ Turn off Retweets

✉ 🔔⁺ **Following**

Dana Stoloff Re
@StoloffDana Follows

⊙ View Topics

Company

Dana Stoloff is here to serves the overall Brov

📋 Add/remove from Lists ◄◄◄◄ eeds. Dana proudly

📅 Joined December 2

📋 View Lists

103 Following   **80** Fc

Followed by Will

🎗 View Moments

ealtor and 23 others you follow

Tweets

🔗 Copy link to profile

Media   Likes

Dana Stoloff
Keepin' It Rea

🔇 Mute @StoloffDana

pany @StoloffDana 6h ⌄

Is the Health
The pandemic

🚫 Block @StoloffDana

an Areas?
amine the components that

Here you can add Dana to one of my lists, copy link to profile, mute or block him.

Thank you for purchasing my Learn to be a Twitter Expert book. After you have studied the book I am sure you will want to further your education on Twitter. You probably didn't realize all that goes into building your account. I have a 90 minute teaching course which is 4 videos that covers some of the subjects in this e-book and more. So you can have a better understanding of Twitter and its benefits

$19.00

I also manage twitter accounts on a month to month basis. It can get your account snowballing forward

$39 a month

Click menu: Twitter Training Course

www.collectbackrent.com

www.ingramcontent.com/pod-product-compliance
Lightning Source LLC
Chambersburg PA
CBHW030534220526
45463CB00007B/2832